CW00734463

JP

1, 2 & 3 John

WALKING IN THE TRUTH

CWR

Claire Musters

Contents

Introduction

About John

We aren't told precisely who the author of 1, 2 and 3 John was – the first letter is anonymous and the writer of the other two simply calls himself 'the elder'. However, all three letters are widely believed to have been written by the same John who wrote both the Gospel of John and the book of Revelation. John was the disciple that 'Jesus loved' (John 21:20) – this is an important point because he had been a close friend of Jesus', which we will see is vital to the message in his letters. Scholars believe the letters were written around AD 90 from Ephesus, after John wrote his Gospel but before he was exiled to Patmos (where he wrote Revelation). Churches had been popping up all over the place due to the gospel spreading rapidly (often due to huge persecution). But John wrote his letters in response to a big problem that seemed to be affecting many of the churches.

John was old by this point; the only remaining original disciple alive, and probably also one of the last eye-witnesses to all Jesus had done. He could see how second and third generation Christians were being swayed by the rise of false teaching. The writings of the apostles, such as Paul, were beginning to be circulated, but, because the apostles themselves were no longer around, it was difficult to have careful oversight over all the churches. There were more travelling teachers too. This opened people up to falling prey to following teaching that seemed logical and attractive but did not align with biblical truth.

Cultural thinking and Gnosticism

Some of the general widespread cultural opinions were beginning to seep into the Church. Gnosticism was rife; this term covers a variety of beliefs but at its core is the notion that everything spiritual is good and everything physical is evil.

There was an emphasis on knowledge, as Gnostics believed certain individuals possessed spiritual knowledge (*gnosis*) that enabled those who grasped hold of it to, at death, pass freely back to their spiritual states and be reunited with God. This teaching was attractive to intellectuals as it seemed to go beyond the simple approach of the apostles. Gnostics also believed that Jesus couldn't possibly have been a man, which resulted in Docetism – the idea that He was in fact a spirit.

People were finding it difficult to believe that Jesus was both fully God and fully human. False teaching upheld that 'the Christ' only came upon Jesus at His baptism but left again before His death on the cross (Cerinthianism). This was because Gnostics believed that it was impossible for the Christ, a spiritual being, to experience suffering of any kind. As we will see, however, John makes the vital point that a human could not be a once-for-all sacrifice and so this distorted teaching negates the work of Jesus on the cross and leaves us with empty religion. John was at pains to continually describe how Jesus is the means of our salvation.

Gnostics had a mixed relationship with their bodies; some treated them badly, as punishment for being evil, while others became promiscuous and over-indulgent, asserting that sins committed by the body were not important as only the spirit mattered. Such teaching creeping into the Church alarmed John, and there are many parallels with world-views and their effects on church beliefs today.

Purpose of John's letters
John wrote his letters with clarity and purpose, determined to ensure that all Christians would know and follow the truth. His authority came from the fact that he had walked and talked with Jesus and watched His ministry, death and resurrection so could bear witness to it all. The first letter is the longest and it is believed to have been written to be

circulated around many churches, whereas the second and third are much shorter and were originally for specific people or places. As well as addressing false teaching, the common themes throughout all three letters are truth, life, light and love. In each letter, John also included simple and practical explanations of what it means to be in relationship with God and how to continue walking in the truth of that relationship. John uses similar imagery to that found in the Gospel of John, and again utilises many contrasts such as light and darkness, God and Satan, love and hate.

Most scholars agree that it is difficult to impose a structure on John's letters – particularly the first. It is best to view 1 John as spiralling and repetitive, rather than linear; each time John reintroduces a theme, it is to give a new perspective or to go deeper into the truth of what it means. While some have commented that he was a very old man by this point, so could have been forgetful, he writes with a passion and authority that shows he is desperate for Christians to truly grasp hold of the truth. As we will be working through the letters in a systematic way, you will therefore come across some repetition in the chapters of this book.

John desperately wanted to encourage Christians to continue to walk faithfully in the truth of their salvation. This encouragement is something we continue to need today, so I hope that this study guide will help to spur you on as you work through it, either as an individual or in a group setting.

WEEK ONE

God is light

1 John 1

Opening Icebreaker

As a group, talk about situations where members have been in total darkness. (For example, inside a cave with all the lights switched off.) What were people's feelings about being in pitch blackness? How did people feel when the lights were switched back on?

Bible Readings

- 1 John 1
- John 1:1–15
- John 3:19–21
- John 17

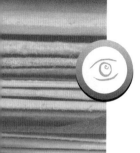

Opening Our Eyes

John begins his first letter strongly, although, 'That which was from the beginning' (1 John 1:1), does not seem like a normal start of a letter to our modern eyes. However, John is setting out the basis for writing straight away; to assert that the person of Jesus *was* God incarnate. This opening phrase is similar to that found in his Gospel, 'In the beginning was the Word, and the Word was with God, and the Word was God. He was with God in the beginning,' (John 1:1–2) as well as the start of the Bible itself, 'In the beginning God created the heavens and the earth' (Gen. 1:1). John is showing us that, as far back as we can imagine, Jesus was there with His Father, and that the Word of life made flesh was the same eternal being. The term 'That which' may seem an odd way to describe a person, but he also includes human sensory words such as 'seen', 'looked' and 'touched' to show how the Word, *logos*, is both the eternal revelation of God and a person he knew personally.

The heresies beginning to infiltrate the Church could only get a foothold if John's witness accounts were discredited. So it is vital that, in the first few verses, John keeps reiterating that his readers can have confidence in his testimony because he spent time with Jesus. In verse three, John reveals the purpose of his writing: to proclaim the truth of 'what we have seen and heard' in order that his readers could have fellowship with one another – and, most importantly, with Jesus. John is doing what Jesus commanded His disciples to do in Matthew 28:19–20.

The life that John describes in verse two is defined by this relationship, which echoes Jesus' words: 'Now this is eternal life: that they know you, the only true God, and Jesus Christ, whom you have sent' (John 17:3). Sharing the truth was to bring John, and his readers, great joy. This should be a natural consequence of having faith in Jesus Christ. While John may have had face to face fellowship with Jesus, a close relationship with Him is open to us all (see John 20:29).

John's letter states some big theological truths about who God is. The first one is found in verse five, where he declares that God is light. John often uses simple propositions to convey profound truths (see, for example, John 4:24 where he simply says that 'God is spirit'). Light is associated with God throughout Scripture, and reflects His goodness, purity and holiness. John moves on to describe how the fact that God is light should affect us as we seek to walk in that light. He makes the imagery of light come alive even more by contrasting it with darkness. He has a dig at some of the false teaching by asserting the truth and then revealing how preposterous it is to believe we can be walking in the truth, while actually stumbling around in darkness.

John then uses another set of contrasting imagery – sin and forgiveness. Those who confess Jesus is Lord have His light constantly shining into their hearts, exposing any sin lurking there. While some false teachers were claiming to be sinless, the Bible makes it clear that, 'all have sinned and fall short of the glory of God' (Rom. 3:23). The truth that fills our hearts with joy is found in verse nine of 1 John 1: that Jesus is able to both forgive *and* purify us from our sins. There is a condition though – we must recognise and confess our sins. John ends by using a shock tactic – that if we claim we have not sinned, we are basically calling Jesus a liar.

Discussion Starters

1. The Greek word for fellowship used in verse three is *koinoia*, which was often used to describe marriage. Why do you think John chose this particular word?

    _____

    _____

    _____

2. Read John 17 together. How is John continuing the work that Jesus started in the first chapter of 1 John?

    _____

    _____

    _____

3. Light is a symbol for God throughout the Bible. Look at some examples together and discuss how God is represented as light in them.

    _____

    _____

    _____

    _____

4. 1 John 1 talks about walking out our faith, which indicates a persistent lifestyle. How can we ensure we do this?

    _____

    _____

    _____

    _____

5. False teachers were minimising or redefining sin, but the Bible is clear that God holds us accountable for our sins. Look up some examples in the Bible where the issue of sin is addressed and discuss them.

6. Read 2 Samuel 11–13. How did David try to cover up his sins? What was his response when confronted? What did he lose as a result of his sin?

7. Sin, confession and repentance are not popular preaching topics. Why do you think that is? Think about how your church encourages confession and what else it could be doing.

8. Discuss honestly what your response is when God's light exposes something in your life.

Personal Application

John wanted his readers to be totally clear about Jesus' true identity. We need to be clear on this today too. The world is full of 'truth' based on personal opinion. Our culture tells us that whatever we believe to be true is fine for us to label as truth. However, we can end up making God to be the way we want Him to be. But we cannot have fellowship with Him when we refuse to accept God as He is and do not allow ourselves to be exposed to the light.

Jesus called us 'the light of the world' and instructed us to 'let your light shine before others, that they may see your good deeds and glorify your Father in heaven' (Matt. 5:14,16). Are we certain of what we believe, and are we walking in the light of it?

Seeing Jesus in the Scriptures

John continually reminded his readers that the message he was sharing, he had heard from Jesus Himself. We can see this is true in regards to God being light. Jesus Himself said in John 8:12, 'I am the light of the world. Whoever follows me will never walk in darkness, but will have the light of life.' He makes it even clearer that He and God are one in John 12: 'Whoever believes in me does not believe in me only, but in the one who sent me. The one who looks at me is seeing the one who sent me. I have come into the world as a light, so that no one who believes in me should stay in darkness' (vv44–46).

WEEK TWO

Commanded to love
1 John 2

Opening Icebreaker

Have a think about what it is that reveals the fact that a child belongs to their parents.

Bible Readings

- 1 John 2
- Matthew 22:34–40
- Romans 3:21–26
- 1 Corinthians 13
- Philippians 3
- James 4

Opening Our Eyes

In this chapter, John starts by explaining that he writes so that his readers will not sin. But he then reminds us of the wonderful news; when we *do* sin, we have an advocate. Jesus' sacrifice was once-for-all. The use of the term 'Righteous One' emphasises the dual nature of Jesus again. As God, He is righteous by definition, but Hebrews 4:15 reminds us that He was totally without sin as a human too. This is how He is able to speak to God on our behalf.

John then goes on to talk about a commandment that has been around since the days of the Law (see Lev. 19:18, Deut. 6:5) but has been made new in Jesus. While He confirmed the old commandment to love (see Matt. 22:34–40), He also interpreted it in a new, radical way (see John 13:34 and 15:13). Love is seen as a by-product of the new life that we have in Him (as well as a sign of maturity), not a duty.

In verses 12–14, which is set out as poetry, John addresses children first, then fathers and then young men. Some say that these are referring to three different age groups in the church, but it seems more likely that the groups are levels of maturity. 'Little children' are those who have recently received forgiveness through Jesus (or those still very immature), 'fathers' are the mature Christians and the 'young men' are those becoming mature through effective use of the Word of God. Each 'because' phrase is a certain truth that he wants them to take hold of.

John talks next about a type of love that God does not want us to have – love of the world. The word 'world' sometimes stands for the beauty of God's creation (see 1 Chron. 16:30–33; Psa. 24:1) but at other times to that which is in opposition to God (Satan is sometimes called the prince of this world – see John 14:30). It is the latter meaning that John is using here, stating that if we love the world we cannot love the Father (James says this too in James 4). John describes three ways that this world can entice us in verse 16; all relate to normal and natural appetites that we are tempted to satisfy in forbidden ways. That is the same strategy the devil has been using since the beginning of the earth (see Gen. 3 and Matt. 4:1–11). It is so important to remember that this world is ultimately wasting away and that we should fix our focus on God. I have been a Christian for a long time, but there are still moments when I have to use the Word of God to combat feelings of rejection from others. I really value deep connections – but I also know the deepest connection we can ever have is with God!

We are still in the 'last hour' that John refers to (the time between Jesus' first and second comings). John is the only biblical author to use the expression 'antichrist', although Jesus warned of false prophets (see Matt. 24:24) and Paul spoke about a man of lawlessness (2 Thess. 2:3–4). *Anti* means 'against, or instead of, and John is warning of those 'false Christs' that Jesus spoke of. We shouldn't be surprised when there are people advocating, or setting themselves up as, false Christs. But we *can* hold on to the truth through faith in Jesus, through the anointing of the Holy Spirit and through actively choosing to love one another.

Discussion Starters

1. Jesus was the ultimate sacrifice; God's way of meeting the penalty of sin so He could commune with us. Take some time to study both Old Testament and New Testament passages together to learn more about Jesus' once-for-all atoning sacrifice.

2. Take a look at the Ten Commandments and then discuss how Jesus interpreted them even more radically.

3. How has Jesus both fulfilled the Law and also superseded it?

4. There are over 100 instances of the phrase 'one another' in the New Testament, a third of those about loving one another. Take some time to look up some examples and discuss how you can love one another practically.

5. Jesus had perfect obedience to God's will – how did He carry that out in practice?

_____

_____

_____

_____

6. Take a look at Genesis 3. How did the way the snake tempted Eve reflect the three ways the world entices us, as described by John?

_____

_____

_____

_____

7. John tells us that we have received God's anointing. Take some time to look through the Bible to see how anointing was used throughout Scripture.

_____

_____

_____

_____

8. What does John say about persevering in our faith?

_____

_____

_____

_____

Personal Application

There are three ways we can be lured away from the command to love God:

- The lust of the flesh – while our bodies are not sinful, our corrupt nature can grip hold of us and we crave certain things such as sex, food and alcohol (see Gal. 5:17–23).

- The lust of the eyes – surrounded by advertising, we need to avoid the trap of 'I can see it, I like it and therefore I am going to have it'. We can be pressurised into thinking like the world, but the Bible tells us to renew our minds (see Rom. 12:2).

- Pride of life – we can look at what we have, or what we have achieved, and believe that it is all down to us. But *everything* we have is a gift from God (see 1 Cor. 4:7).

Take some time to think about how you can avoid being lured away from God.

Seeing Jesus in the Scriptures

Jesus' love attracted all types of people to Him. His disciples misunderstood Him, blundered around and even abandoned Him. And yet He lovingly taught them, revealed the Father's heart to them (John 14–16), prayed for them (John 17) and commissioned them to continue His work (Matt. 28:20). Learning from Jesus' example, and submitting to His leadership in our lives will teach us how to love like He does. In verse 28 of 1 John 2, John reminds us to always 'continue in him', much as Jesus says Himself in John 15. As we do this, we will bear much fruit – the first of which is love (see Gal. 5:22–23).

WEEK THREE

Children of God

1 John 3

Opening Icebreaker

As a group, talk about times when members have experienced power cuts in their homes or at work. How have they managed without electricity?

Bible Readings

- 1 John 3
- Romans 6–8
- Genesis 4:1–16
- John 15

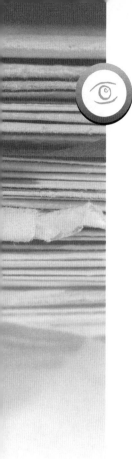

Opening Our Eyes

I love the opulence of the phrase 'the Father has lavished on us' in the first verse of 1 John 3. It speaks to me of how God has purposefully and freely poured His outrageous love onto each of us. I find it a great verse to meditate on in difficult moments. The themes covered in this chapter are not new, but here they relate to our relationship to God. This is the reason we can have a sense of security, why the world doesn't recognise us and why we are willing to purify ourselves under His loving, careful hand. It is amazing to ponder the fact that God initiated this love relationship in the first place. It wasn't down to us at all; God had already provided a means for our salvation through Jesus. Placing this truth straight after chapters on God's light and holiness makes it all the more mind-blowing!

John continues by saying that our identity as children of God should be reflected in our lifestyles. He isn't saying that we will never sin (see 1 John 1:8–10; 2:1) but that it is an attitude of the heart. As sin is an act of lawlessness, those who practise it become lawless. When a Christian deliberately sins over and over again, the work of the cross is belittled (see Rom. 6–8 for more on sin, the Law, Jesus' death and resurrection). As God's children, the natural result of spending time with Him is that we begin to sin less as our faith begins to grow.

John uses a series of contrasts in verses 7–10 to build up a picture of those who live as children of God and those who don't. Those with little experience, the children (or new generation of believers) with their trusting natures, could be easily led astray, so John gives instructions on how to discern between children of God and children of the devil. While we may look at personality, it is all about character (as Jesus taught in Matt. 7:15–16).

Verse 10 introduces John's next point: our responsibility as children of God. Love is not true love until it is put into action. Again, John uses contrasting figures to bring home his point. Cain's story is followed by Jesus', juxtaposing one whose offering cost him nothing and whose heart was full of hate, with one whose sacrifice was perfect. I am reminded of King David too, who said that he would never offer a sacrifice that cost him nothing (2 Sam. 24:24). I try to remember this on the mornings when I am exhausted but am required to lead worship. Knowing that my sacrifice shows my love for God and His Church, helps me to focus on serving with the right attitude. Verse 17 in particular is extremely practical – and challenging!

As the chapter closes, John gives his readers assurance of how we can know we are children of God. It is true that our hearts know all our hidden motives, but God knows us even better. If we stop dwelling on the feeling that we aren't good enough, and start dwelling more on His unwavering love and acceptance, the natural result will be a motivation to live in a way that pleases Him. I have certainly found this to be the case in my own life.

While faith may be costly, the reward is everlasting life with our Father! It is also simple: we just need to believe in the triune God. The Holy Spirit is spoken of by name for the first time here: it is through His guidance that we can begin to exhibit family characteristics that show we are children of God.

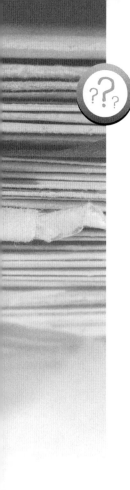

Discussion Starters

1. Ask each person to share something about what the phrase 'child of God' means to them personally.

2. Our experiences with our parents can colour how we view our relationship with our heavenly Father. Talk about the positive and negative implications of this.

3. As children of God we enjoy the same inheritance as Jesus. Romans 8 talks about us being adopted. Discuss what you know about Roman adoption laws and what this can tell us about our standing before God.

4. Romans 6–7 contrasts being slaves to sin and slaves to righteousness. Discuss some of the points that strike you and how they relate to what we have been learning in 1 John 3.

5. What spiritual disciplines are useful for our inner spiritual nature?

_____

_____

_____

_____

6. As we see in verse 23, faith and love are often grouped together. Look up some other examples and discuss the relationship between faith and love.

_____

_____

_____

_____

7. Read through Cain and Abel's story (Gen. 4:1–16) together, and discuss what you can learn about heart attitude, how anger can turn to hate etc.

_____

_____

_____

_____

8. How does knowing that we are children of God shedlight on the command to share what we have with others?

_____

_____

_____

_____

Personal Application

Verse 2 is so exciting – our identity as God's children is already settled – and yet there is so much more that we have to experience! Throughout our lives God is making us more and more like Jesus (Rom. 8:29). Isn't that amazing? Knowing we are children of God can anchor us in times of distress and should stop us from being complacent. It can be helpful to occasionally ponder our motives. Are we trying to impress those around us? Do we feel pressurised by others into doing things we 'ought to'? Or is our service to others a natural overflow of gratitude for the love our Father has lavished on us?

Seeing Jesus in the Scriptures

John encourages his readers to look to the actions of others (the fruit of their lives) to see whether they are children of God (Jesus' own life reflected who He was, see Acts 10:38). He also had some choice words to say to the Jewish leaders who thought highly of themselves, and yet were setting themselves up against Him (see John 8:31–47). Jesus commanded His disciples to love one another (John 15:12). The only way that this is possible is because of His incredible sacrifice of love for us. He set His face to be 'obedient to death – even death on a cross!' (Phil. 2:8). This is how we have become co-heirs with Christ (Rom. 8:17) and how we are able overcome sin and live as sons and daughters of God (see Rom. 8:9–13).

WEEK FOUR

God is love

1 John 4

Opening Icebreaker

Pour water into a jug so that it is three-quarters full and then get a member of the group to place a glass inside of it so it is also filled with water. How might this illustrate God's love to and in us?

Bible Readings

- 1 John 4
- John 10
- John 17:20–26
- Hebrews 9–10:18

Opening Our Eyes

We have already seen how John asserted that God is light (1 John 1:5); in this fourth chapter he makes another equally short but strong statement – God is love (1 John 4:8). John has already talked a lot about love in his letter, but here he is going to the very essence of it. In previous chapters, he's written to his readers about what God has done for us *because* of His love; but here the focus is that this *is* Him. God *is* love.

John believes we need this full understanding of the source of all love, because we ourselves have been commanded to love. He explains that true love is never static – God sent His *'one and only* Son' to us to die on the cross (v9). That is the enormity of God's love. John reminds his readers that all love begins – and ends – in God. If it were not for His love, we would all be lost, with no hope of redemption. The term 'atoning sacrifice' is used again in this chapter (v10). Some say that a loving God would never have asked for such a sacrifice, but this would refute the fact that God is also light, holiness and purity. And love actually manifests itself in acts of self-sacrifice – Jesus' was the ultimate act of perfect love.

We are given the privilege of loving, because of God's love. The amazing thing is our loving one another makes His love complete in us (v12) and we can also be confident of our future (v17), even on the day of judgment.

The concept of us living in God and Him living in us is repeated four times. John knew this was quite difficult to grasp, particularly because we can't see God (v12) as He is Spirit (John 4:24), and so he reminds his readers of three witnesses they can be sure of: the apostles' testimony (v14), personal acknowledgement that Jesus is the Son of God (v15) and through the receiving of the Holy Spirit (v13).

The famous verse 'perfect love drives out fear' is found in this chapter (v18). If we think God is standing over us waiting to punish us when we do something wrong, then we do not yet have a correct understanding of His love. The devil, of course, is more than happy to keep telling us this lie, because it gives us a warped view of God's love.

The chapter actually begins with an encouragement to 'test the spirits' (v1). Just as the devil likes to warp our view of God, he also likes to counterfeit His teaching too. As we've seen, this was happening within the churches John was writing to. His words warn us not to be naïve, simply lapping up everything we hear without weighing it. He gives us some pointers as to how to test what is said to us: is it denying that Jesus is the Son of God (vv1–3)? Is it encouraging us to worship God or leading us to fix our gaze elsewhere? False teachers reflect the world's view (v5), which makes them popular, whereas true apostles are known by what they teach (v6). While some teaching panders to whatever is in vogue currently, the real truth is not something that can be changed – it is defined by the character of God.

John also reminds us that we are overcomers (v4). We have no need to be fearful because we have the power of Jesus within us.

Discussion Starters

1. Using Hebrews 9 and 10, discuss how Jesus made God known to people, and how His sacrifice did away with the need for ceremonial sacrifices.

   _____

   _____

   _____

   _____

2. Take some time to discuss how God's love differs from our culture's ideas of what love is.

   _____

   _____

   _____

   _____

3. If we reveal God's love to the world through the way that we love one another, can you give a few practical examples of how this can happen?

   _____

   _____

   _____

   _____

4. In 1 Timothy 4:12, Paul encourages Timothy to set an example in love to those around him. How well do you think your group is doing this? What example are you setting to the rest of your church and to those outside the Church?

   _____

   _____

   _____

   _____

5. 1 John 4:16 talks about relying on God's love – what does that mean to you practically?

_____

_____

_____

_____

6. Take some time to think about the inheritance that we will receive and how this is already revealing God's love to us in what we can enjoy of it today.

_____

_____

_____

_____

7. How did fear manifest itself in Adam and Eve (see Gen. 3), and what did that do to their relationship with God?

_____

_____

_____

_____

8. If there is no fear in love, why do you think so many of us still struggle with fear?

_____

_____

_____

_____

Personal Application

It is incredible to ponder the fact that God was burning with love for us long before we ever started to love Him! If we find that difficult to comprehend, or accept, for ourselves, meditating on 1 John 3:1–2 is helpful. In 1 John 4:12, we read how it is the love between Christians that reveals the love of the Father to the world – what an awesome responsibility! We can talk about loving God, but be quick to criticise other Christians. If our love for each other is how God has chosen to show His love to the world, then we need to ask ourselves honestly if we need to repent on this issue. If you know there is someone in your church that you find difficult to love, why don't you ask God to reveal to you *His* love for that person?

Seeing Jesus in the Scriptures

All definitions of love stem from Jesus' single, definitive act on the cross. In John 10, Jesus gives His perspective, stating that He willingly laid down His life (vv17–18). He is our practical example of what love is. Jesus also likens Himself to a shepherd who lays down his life for his sheep. This gives us another indication of how we can recognise false teaching; if we believe Jesus is God's Son and cultivate a relationship with Him, we begin to recognise His voice (see vv14–16). He also prayed that we would be one, as that is how the world would recognise Him (John 17:20–23).

WEEK FIVE

Faith and life

1 John 5

Opening Icebreaker

In pairs, get people to take it in turns to fall backwards while the other person catches them. (Please remember that this is optional and only suitable for those physically able.)

Bible Readings

- 1 John 5
- John 11
- Matthew 3:13–17
- Ephesians 2:1–10
- Hebrews 11

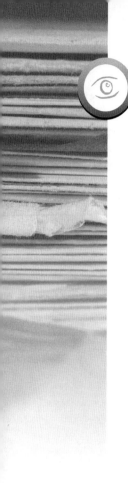

Opening Our Eyes

There are many familiar themes in chapter five, as it does act somewhat as a summary for the letter, although, yet again, the perspective is slightly different. Here John concentrates on the vital elements of our faith, using the phrase, 'everyone who' again and again. As he comes to the last part of his letter, he re-emphasises how we can be assured of our faith – by believing in Jesus as the Son of God. Everyone who 'believes' is born of God. The tenses used in the original Greek, indicate that this belief is actually a present and continuing reality. The amazing truth is that this faith was both initiated by God (Eph. 2:4) and is a gift from Him (Eph. 2:8).

Verses 2–3 reveal how love, obedience and victory are evidence of our faith in Jesus. John loves to use the word 'overcome' and here we see our victory is the result of faith. And faith comes through hearing 'the message' (Rom. 10:17), learning more about Jesus and our understanding of our position as children of God.

In the rest of this chapter, John gives us five certainties that we can build our lives upon.

1. Jesus *is* God: John mentions three witnesses that refuted the claims that Jesus was either simply a liar or just a man, rather than God Himself. Jesus 'came by water and blood' (v6) – this was refuting the false teaching that Jesus was only 'The Christ' between His baptism and death. Indeed God testified at His baptism as to who He was (Matt. 3:13–17). The Holy Spirit also testifies (see John 15:26; 16:14).

2. Eternal life: By believing in Jesus we also have everlasting life in Him. This reminds us that we do not have to (and cannot) earn it. It can only be received.

3. God answers prayer: In verse 15, John asserts that we
will receive whatever we ask of God. We may not see it
immediately, but we can be assured that God answers
prayers submitted to His will.

4. Christians do not habitually sin: We are reminded
here again that, while none of us are perfect, it is about
attitude. If we are God's, then we are free from the
clutches of sin – and we can pray for one another when
we do fall prey to temptation. John does talk about a sin
that 'leads to death' here. It can be confusing to unpack
this (as in Rom. 6:23 we are told that the wages of all sin
is death) and yet the whole passage (in fact the whole
letter) is about believing Jesus is the Son of God and
refuting those false teachers that were saying otherwise.
So this sin is probably about those who deny God's
saving truth. Any who are preaching such falsity, and
those who leave the church to follow them, are turning
their backs on their means for salvation.

5. Awareness of God's truth and presence: John comes
full circle back to the fellowship with God that he first
mentions in chapter one of his first letter. We can know
the truth through what the Son teaches us.

John's final word is about idols. As he was probably writing
to believers from Ephesus, this was a very real warning
about how, while their culture may have been given over to
the worship of idols at the temple of Diana, idols are not real
and are a waste of time. In fact, anything that pushes God
out of His rightful place in the centre of our hearts is an idol –
a sobering thought...

Discussion Starters

1. What does the story of Lazarus in John 11 teach us about life only being found in God?

2. What does saying we love God while disobeying Him reveal about our attitude towards God Himself?

3. Read Hebrews 11 together. Take some time to discuss what the chapter teaches you about active faith.

4. Look at Jesus' teaching in the Gospels to see what He said about God's commands (for example, in Matt. 11).

5. In Jesus we are given life. Look up the following scriptures and discuss what life in the Son means to you personally: John 5:21,26,40; 17:2–3.

6. What are some of the things that can actually hinder our prayers from being heard by God?

7. What can we learn about our approach to prayer through Jesus' own example?

8. Why do you think that some of our prayers can seem to take a long time to be answered?

Personal Application

This last chapter pulls together the encouragement found throughout the letter: to be sure of our hope in Jesus. The more we get to know Him, the more deeply we will love Him and become like Him. The love for others, obedience and victory that we can see in our lives are simply by-products of our faith in Him. Why do we struggle with these things, then? Sometimes we forget to see things through God's eternal perspective. For example, the truth is that we are now in the kingdom of light so the enemy has no hold on us. Our faith is not the means of our victory – Jesus' death is. Despite what we see around us; we need to remind ourselves that Jesus has won the ultimate victory (see John 16:33).

Seeing Jesus in the Scriptures

As the heart of this letter is to remind its readers that our faith is based on the belief that Jesus is the Son of God, let's unpack the three witnesses of who Jesus is a little more, as they are the testimony of God rather than of man (v9).

- The water – in Matthew 3:13–17, the Spirit descended upon Jesus at His baptism and God Himself stated that Jesus is His Son.

- The blood – in John 12:28 Jesus predicted His death. At that time, God again testified.

- The Holy Spirit – as we have already seen, Jesus said that the Spirit testifies as to who He is. He remains a witness to our hearts today (see Rom. 8:15–16).

WEEK SIX

Be alert

2 John

Opening Icebreaker

Ask those in the group to share a time when perhaps they weren't as attentive to a situation as they should have been, and the subsequent problems that arose.

Bible Readings

- 2 John
- John 14:15–21
- Mark 13
- 2 Corinthians 11:2–4

Opening Our Eyes

Some commentators believe 2 John was written to a specific woman while others assert that it was aimed at a particular church, which perhaps met in the lady's home. There is certainly a feeling of both family and congregation in this letter. It is important to recognise that family (both our own and the Church) can be targeted by the enemy, but we have spiritual armour to enable us to fight his schemes (see Eph. 6). In my family, we often find our children's behaviour takes a nosedive on the Sundays that I am leading worship and my husband is preaching. We have come to realise that this is not a coincidence and cover our family, and church, in even more prayer those days.

In 2 John, the command to love appears in verses 4–6, where it is emphasised as an old teaching. While the letter is full of friendship and joy, the overall message is to remain alert to false teaching. John begins by stressing how vital the truth is (the word 'truth' appears four times in the first three verses). The truth that Jesus is the Son of God was being compromised by false teachers. Perhaps, as well, some of the Early Church had a very laidback attitude to the truth (verse 4 talks of *some* walking in the truth). The New International Version of the Bible starts a new paragraph with verse seven, but John is continuing on from his previous point: 'I say this *because…*' By linking the two sections, he is reminding them of the call to obedience and love precisely because Christians were beginning to be deceived. Loving one another is a great weapon against deceit.

John is very clear about opposing error, which appears to have 'gone out' from those previously within a church (v7). He gives a stark warning to his readers, telling them not to lose what they already had by entertaining the notions of the false teachers. Anyone who goes outside of Jesus' teaching is not a child of God's. There were many who enjoyed listening to the latest ideas (Acts 17:21) but John reminds them that, while God has given us intellect and imagination, if we run ahead of Him we are in danger of accepting lies as truth. He was not discouraging growth and progress (John 16:12–15; 2 Pet. 3:18) but reminding readers that our plumb line should always be the Word of God. We also have the witness of the Holy Spirit inside of us (2 Tim. 1:13–14).

John goes so far as to say that anyone who welcomes false teachers into their homes shares in what they are doing. That may seem harsh, but there were not many inns in which travelling teachers could stay in safety and so churches were used to offering hospitality. Yet if the church sheltered false teachers, they were opening themselves up to falling prey to believing lies. It could sway others too, as the teachers would be able to say that this church had accepted them so others would be more likely to. Tolerance may seem to be a positive trait, but not when it puts the truth in jeopardy.

John's letter ends with a desire to talk face to face, and greetings from 'the children of your sister' (v13), which is most likely a sister church. While we need to be careful of false teaching, we should never isolate ourselves – being connected to other churches helps facilitate unity and also brings encouragement and correction where necessary.

Discussion Starters

1. Discuss some of our society's notions of truth and love.

_____

_____

_____

_____

_____

2. Obedience, truth and love are all meshed together in this letter (as in the previous one). How do we ensure we are walking in all three daily?

_____

_____

_____

_____

_____

3. John warns against losing what has been gained, and mentions rewards (v8). Take some time to look through Matthew 25:14–28 and 1 Corinthians 3:12–15 and discuss the concept of rewards.

_____

_____

_____

_____

_____

4. Why do you think that Christians can fall prey to false teachers?

_____

_____

_____

_____

_____

5. Read Matthew 7:15–23 together and discuss why you think Jesus said that there will be those who come to Him saying 'Lord' who He will turn away.

_____

_____

_____

_____

_____

6. In Peter 2:2 we are told there will be many deceivers. How do you think we can guard against them in our own lives, and in our churches?

_____

_____

_____

_____

_____

7. John talks about refusing hospitality to false teachers. Do you think this can be a justification for divisions in the Church (such as between denominations)? Why or why not?

_____

_____

_____

_____

_____

8. In an age of instant, digital communication, do you think face to face interaction is still important?

_____

_____

_____

_____

_____

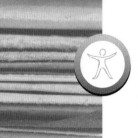

Personal Application

Being alert to the attacks on biblical truth seems like a very apt message for today. We live in a society where truth is becoming more relative – one person's truth is not another's. That way of thinking has crept into some churches too, which we need to be aware of. This does not mean that we should only converse with those we agree with, as we should love all our brothers and sisters. But John is talking about issues of salvation and the necessity of believing who Jesus is – we need to guard that truth at all costs.

I like how the letter ends with greetings from another church. If this church was meeting in a woman's home it may have been fairly small. I personally know that when we started a church we so appreciated the love and support from other churches we were in relationship with. How can you encourage other churches in your community?

Seeing Jesus in the Scriptures

John was not the only one who emphasised the need to stay alert. In Mark 13, Jesus warns that there will be many false teachers who claim to come in His name. He also says that no person knows when He will return, so we need to keep ourselves ready and prepared. We do not want to be found sleeping, as His disciples were in Matthew 26:36–46. His response to them is a challenge to us today too: 'Watch and pray so that you will not fall into temptation. The spirit is willing, but the flesh is weak' (v41).

WEEK SEVEN

Stay faithful

3 John

Opening Icebreaker

Ask if anyone has any stories of friends and family (or even pets!) showing an unusually high level of faithfulness.

Bible Readings

- 3 John
- 1 Corinthians 3–4
- Philippians 2:1–11; 3

Opening Our Eyes

John's third letter is another short one, and, although it has many of the same elements in it that appear in the other two, it is the most personal of all. It was written to encourage a particular individual, Gaius. The themes within it reflect what is happening within the church he is a part of. John has a fatherly concern for all those that could be involved in what seems to be a power struggle, as one person is dominating events in the congregation. It seems there is a battle going on for the truth. There are three characters mentioned in the letter, who we will look at in turn.

Gaius was a 'dear friend' of John's – indeed his opening remarks offer personal prayers for Gaius' physical as well as spiritual health. This was also refuting the popular heresy that physical and spiritual were separate (and the physical despised). John indicates that Gaius is a faithful follower who shows great love and hospitality to his fellow believers – particularly the travelling speakers. While in the previous letter John spoke about not welcoming false teachers, here he is at great pains to encourage Gaius in his hospitality, as the true teachers who travelled around to various churches needed those who would open their homes, and hearts, to them. Gaius had been doing this gladly, and John reiterates that by doing so, he is in fact becoming an active part in their ministry.

This picture of a faithful friend is contrasted by the description of Diotrephes, who seems to have set himself up as a leader. He has already stopped the church from welcoming John (v9). It appears that John had written to Diotrephes first but felt the need to also write to Gaius to make his friend aware of what was going on (and encourage him to persevere if he was experiencing similar difficulties with Diotrephes – see Gal. 6:9). While it is not clear exactly what Diotrephes had done, we can see that pride and a desire for control were motivating factors in his actions (v9). He was also spreading lies about John and other teachers and getting rid of anyone who wouldn't conform to his way of thinking. The expansion of the Church and the rapid way it was growing must have meant that there was some fluidity between the way the church leaders and the apostles governed together. And this seems to have opened up some problems in this particular church. Whether Diotrephes was a church leader or simply a domineering member who felt his way was the only way, it was his ambition that had determined his negative actions. Paul seemed to come up against a similar problem within the Corinthian church (see 1 Cor. 4).

John again uses contrast – the good in Demetrius, our third character, highlights the false in Diotrephes. Demetrius may well have been the person delivering the letter to Gaius. Whoever he was, John commended him for his faithfulness. He was certainly an example of the type of person John would want others to imitate. John finishes the letter by saying that he hopes to see Gaius soon – so perhaps Demetrius had been sent on ahead of John to gather some support in person ready for John's visit.

It is sobering to read about the power struggle in this church, but John was certainly at pains to commend the faithful and deal with the sin being allowed to run riot, illustrating its importance to us.

Discussion Starters

1. John talks about spiritual and physical health in this letter. How can we ensure we keep ourselves healthy in both areas?

_____

_____

_____

_____

_____

2. Would you say hospitality is becoming a lost art in churches? What else does the Bible say about it?

_____

_____

_____

_____

_____

3. How do you view church leadership?

_____

_____

_____

_____

_____

4. How can we spot leaders who are becoming domineering? What action do you think those around them should take?

_____

_____

_____

_____

_____

5. Do you think your church supports its leaders well?

_____

_____

_____

_____

6. In verse 11, John says those who are evil have not seen
God. Yet John 1:18 says _no one_ has seen God... What do
you think he means?

_____

_____

_____

_____

7. Often those who are spoken of well in the Bible, as
Demetrius is, are given to us as examples to imitate (see
Phil. 3:17). How do you think we are meant to do this?

_____

_____

_____

_____

8. Using the three characters within this letter, reflect
on your own discipleship journey towards character
transformation (humbly asking God to reveal both the
positives and negatives).

_____

_____

_____

_____

Personal Application

We have already looked at how there seems to be a battle within our culture over what constitutes truth. This letter shows that wherever there are people, there are going to be difficulties and differences of opinions. We need to ask ourselves whether we are part of the problem or whether we can be part of the solution. No doubt Diotrephes felt totally justified in his actions – this can challenge us to remember to test our own motives regularly and be open to correction.

In our seemingly individualistic society, being hospitable can be a way to keep a check on ourselves and our attitudes. Gaius was commended for his hospitality – would that be something John would say about us if he visited our churches today?

Seeing Jesus in the Scriptures

Interestingly, this is the only New Testament book that doesn't mention Jesus by name. Rather He is called 'the Name' (v7). Put in context, however, this really emphasises the authority Jesus has; He is the motivation for the brothers and sisters going out to proclaim the good news to 'the pagans' (v7). Jesus is referred to as 'the Name' elsewhere in the New Testament (see Acts 5:41) and His power and authority are shown as having been given to Him by God Himself (see Phil. 2:9–11). The passage in Philippians also reminds us of the humility of Jesus, and shows us how He expects the same from us. This is the type of teaching that John no doubt would have been taking to the church in 3 John.

Leader's Notes

These leader's notes have been written to support you as you lead your small group through, what I hope will be, informative and life-giving discussions together.

Week One: God is light

Opening Icebreaker
The point of the discussion is to reflect how light illuminates and how being in the dark can be unsettling.

Discussion Starters

1. The word *koinoia* implies a close relationship – the one we can have with God is the closest we can ever experience. It also has connotations of sharing, participating together, emphasising what is common – all things Christian unity expresses.

2. In John 17, Jesus asserts that He came to earth to reveal the one true God, that He is God's Son (v2) and the way to eternal life. He also confirms that He has shown His disciples the truth. In 1 John 1 the author continually talks about how Jesus was with God from the beginning and that eternal life is found in Him. Both talk about joy being complete in Him too.

3. There are many instances of God as light in the Bible, including:

- God as a pillar of fire – Exodus 13:21.
- Light as God's glory and holiness – Ezekiel 1:4, 27–28; Habakkuk 3:4; 1 Timothy 6:15–16.

- God's presence and favour – Psalm 27:1; 44:3;
  2 Corinthians 4:6.
- God's Word – Psalm 119:105.
- Light as sharing God's wisdom – Isaiah 9:2.

4. Fellowship with other believers is a vital part of being
a Christian (v7), as is delving into the wisdom of God's
Word, confessing our sins and worshipping God for who
He truly is.

5. The main points to get across are that as humans our
nature is sinful so we all fall short of God's standard,
keeping short accounts with God is vital and Jesus is the
way that we can find forgiveness for our sins. Here are
some key points and verses to get you started:

- All are sinful – Isaiah 64:6; Romans 3:23.
- Importance of confession – Proverbs 28:13; Hosea 5:15.
- Helping one another overcome sin – Matthew 18:15;
  Galatians 6:1.
- Forgiving one another's sins – Luke 17:3–4.
- Overcoming sin – Romans 6:14; 1 Corinthians 15:57.
- Jesus is the means by which we can be cleansed of
  sin – Isaiah 53:5; Ephesians 1:7; 2 Corinthians 5:21;
  1 Peter 2:24; Hebrews 9:28.
- Sinfulness ends in death – Romans 6:23.

6. David's first mistake was not looking away, which led
to him taking Bathsheba for himself. Once she was
pregnant, he sent for Uriah to encourage him to sleep
with his wife. When this did not happen, he put him
on the front line. What started as idle looking, ended
in murder. Our sins can start small but can spiral out
of control.

David's sins cost him his peace and joy (see Psa. 32:3,4; Psa. 51), his son (2 Sam. 12:15–19), his family (see 2 Sam. 12:11–12) and almost his kingdom (see later chapters in 2 Sam.). However, he was quick to repent once Nathan pointed out his sin and this restored his relationship with God.

7. They can be seen as somewhat old-fashioned and yet, as the apostles indicated, it is not up to us to 'modernise' biblical concepts.

Facilitate honest discussion about your church's approach to confession – is it helpful or could it do more? Consider further ideas, such as: accountability partnerships, congregational spoken confession and times of silence for individual confession.

8. Allow people a safe place to share. Some may struggle with pride, so their knee-jerk reaction is to be indignant. Others may feel like a failure – remind them of Romans 8:1. Perhaps some may feel that they have tripped up too many times and yet God's mercy is new every morning (Lam. 3:22–23) and He is always willing to forgive those who repent.

Week Two: Commanded to love

Opening Icebreaker
This may include things such as a child looking like their parents, obeying them, showing love to them.

Discussion Starters
1. God's people were given clear instructions about sacrifices (Lev. 1; Ezek. 44). The priests had to make sacrifices day after day, as they did not last. But Jesus'

sacrifice was perfect and did away with the need for continued sacrifices (see Heb. 10). A lamb without blemish was often needed – Jesus was described as the Lamb of God (see John 1:29). Animals were sacrificed involuntarily but His sacrifice was voluntary (Isa. 53:7).

2. Here are the Ten Commandments and New Testament verses to discuss alongside them:
   • Exodus 20:3 and Matthew 4:10
   • Exodus 20:4 and Luke 16:13
   • Exodus 20:7 and Matthew 5:34
   • Exodus 20:8 and Mark 2:27–8
   • Exodus 20:12 and Matthew 10:37
   • Exodus 20:13 and Matthew 5:22
   • Exodus 20:14 and Matthew 5:28
   • Exodus 20:15 and Matthew 5:40
   • Exodus 20:16 and Matthew 12:36
   • Exodus 20:17 and Luke 12:15

   Jesus kept saying, 'You have heard that it was said'... 'But I tell you' – He was taking God's commandments to a new level. His teaching is about heart attitude, rather than simply obeying the Law.

3. John talks about obedience – Jesus also said, 'If you love me, keep my commands' (John 14:15). Jesus also states that He came not to do away with the Law but to fulfil it (Matt. 5:17). And yet His sacrifice did away with the need for continual sacrifice – we are no longer under the Law, but under grace. The Law is no longer written on tablets of stone – but on our hearts (Jer. 31:33 and 2 Cor. 3:13).

4. Here are some verses to get you started:

   • Love one another – John 13:34–35; Romans 13:8; 1 Peter 3:8; 1 John 3:11,23; 4:11–12; 2 John 5.

• Other scriptures – Romans 12:10; Ephesians 4:2; Galatians 5:13.

5. Jesus only did that which He saw His Father doing (John 5:19). Jesus had great compassion on people, ministering to them even when it meant great sacrifice (see Matt. 14:13–21). But He agonised in the Garden of Gethsemane (Matt. 26:36–45). This is a great model for how we can walk closely with our Father too – be honest about our struggles, but ultimately submit to His will.

6. The snake got Eve to question whether God really told her not to eat of the fruit of the tree. Using her natural appetites, the devil pointed out the fruit to Eve that looked so good, she believed it would taste good, but, more than that, the snake also appealed to her pride by telling her she would become like God.

7. In Jesus' time, anointing someone's head with oil was a mark of respect (see Luke 7:46). Here are some examples of this:

• Oil consecrated the offering altar – Exodus 29:36.
• Oil was used to anoint leaders: kings – 1 Samuel 10:1; 16:8–13. priests – Exodus 28:41. prophets – 1 Kings 19:16.
• The anointed one described the awaited Messiah – Daniel 9:25.
• Oil is used to anoint someone who is sick – James 5:14.

When someone was anointed by God for leadership, they were also given power by the Holy Spirit – see 1 Samuel 16:13; Isaiah 61:1. Today each one of us has been anointed (2 Cor. 1:21–22).

8. There are many scripture references about perseverance, such as Hebrews 12:1–3. But John gives us some ideas

in verses 24–29 too where he uses the verb 'remain'
four times:

- Let God's Word remain in us (vv24–25).
- Allow His anointing to teach us (vv26–27).
- Remain in Him – we should root ourselves in Him so we
  are not swayed (v28).

Week Three: Children of God

Opening Icebreaker
The aim of the discussion is to show how being connected to
an energy source makes all the difference. In the same way,
as children of God, we can have access to His power in our
lives constantly.

Discussion Starters
1.　For some, it may bring a sense of security, comfort, joy.
Encourage people to be honest (see below).

2.　While our parents may often have reflected the love of
God in the way they brought us up, none of them will
have been perfect. Sometimes duty and rules are elevated
so much, we can subconsciously feel that we can only
experience God's love if we earn it through good works.

Do not push anyone to talk who seems reluctant to. Be
sensitive to where people are at and, if you are able to,
offer a listening ear outside the group setting (alongside
a counsellor where appropriate).

3.　In Roman law, like ours, an adopted child was entitled to
all the same rights and privileges as a natural-born child.

So this means that we have exactly the same standing before God as Jesus does! (Gal. 4:4–7 may be helpful here too.)

4. Romans 6 highlights how we have been given a new nature, so we no longer need to be slaves to sin (vv5–7). The emphasis on the finished work of Christ giving us power over sin is also mentioned here (vv8–10).

   'Slaves to righteousness' is an interesting term, especially as we are also known as children of God. (We choose to serve our master – see v19 where it says 'offer yourselves'.)

   Romans 7 mentions the Law too, and has a very honest description of what it is like to give in to our sinful nature, even when we are desperately trying not to. It is not that we never sin again; each of us is in a lifelong process of becoming more like Jesus. Just trying to apply knowledge is not enough; we need faith in Jesus and the empowering of the Holy Spirit.

5. We need to keep feeding our inner spiritual nature through the Word of God and conversing with God. But we also need to exercise the spiritual gifts that God has entrusted to us (see Rom. 12 and 1 Cor. 12). This is a way that we can show love to one another. Encourage one another to share what God-given spiritual gifts they have. If anyone finds this difficult, ask the others to help them. CWR also offers a great free resource – search for 'Discovering your basic gift' at cwr.org.uk

6. Here are some examples: John 3:16; Ephesians 1:15; Colossians 1:4; 1 Thessalonians 1:3; 1 Timothy 1:3–5; Galatians 5:6.

Actions should be rooted in love, which is the fruit of faith. Paul saw faith and love as essential indicators of a genuine Christian. Of course, we have faith because of Jesus' love for us too.

7. While the Bible doesn't spell out why God rejected Cain's offering, most commentators believe it is because of his attitude towards the offering. While Abel offered from his first fruits, Cain simply brought 'some of the fruits'.

Cain shows God he is angry, and God warns him he has a choice – to do what is right would have made him acceptable, but caving into temptation turned his anger into murder. (You might want to discuss Jesus' teaching in Matt. 5:22–24 too.)

8. A well-functioning family looks after one another. When one is blessed, they share with those less fortunate – as we see in Acts 2:42–47. When we remember that everything we have comes from our heavenly Father (see 1 Cor. 4:7), how can we not share with others?

Week Four: God is love

Opening Icebreaker
This is a really helpful visual illustration of how we can be 'in God' (the jug of water) and yet He is also 'in us' (the glass).

Discussion Starters
1. The Israelites had to go through all sorts of ceremonies and rituals in order to become close to God (in fact, once the temple was established, it was only the priests who went to the Holy of Holies – just once a year). In that sense, God was somewhat hidden. But Jesus said, 'Anyone who has seen me has seen the Father' (John 14:9). He

was the ultimate priest, and His once-for-all sacrifice did away with the need for continual sacrifices. In fact, Jesus taught that those who loved and obeyed Him would become homes for the Father and Himself (John 14:23).

2. While the world's ideas of love are often based on it being an emotion, God reveals that love is so much more than a feeling. Love is a choice – an action.

3. You could read the passage about Jesus washing His disciples' feet (John 13:1–17), pointing out that He told them to do the same – this is servant-heartedness. You could also discuss 1 Corinthians 12:12–31, as it talks about us being Christ's body. We are on the ground, as it were, God's practical 'hands and feet'. By encouraging one another to use the particular gifts each of us has been given, we enable His body to function as it should.

4. Facilitate an honest discussion on this subject, but try to ensure people are encouraged through it.

5. The verb that is translated in the New International Version as 'rely' comes from the word *pistis*, meaning 'to believe'. It is present tense, which is reflected in the word rely. If we want to learn to rely on God's love we need to understand His character further, through reading His Word. Exercising that belief in His goodness and unending love is important through difficult times, as it is often through our trials that we learn to rely on Him more fully.

6. Here are some scriptures to aid your discussion: Ephesians 1:3; 2:6–7; 1 Corinthians 1:30; Colossians 3:4 and Revelation 21–22.

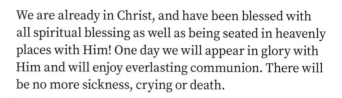

We are already in Christ, and have been blessed with all spiritual blessing as well as being seated in heavenly places with Him! One day we will appear in glory with Him and will enjoy everlasting communion. There will be no more sickness, crying or death.

7. Looking at Genesis 3, talk about the fact that, after they had disobeyed God, fear caused Adam and Eve to hide when God called to them. Fear and pretence, as well as blame shifting, often go together. Perhaps the fear of missing out also lured Eve into eating the apple? Unfortunately, while God gently covered over their nakedness (their fear), this same fear and the resulting actions caused a separation between them.

8. We are all on a journey towards Christlikeness, and so, while Romans 8:1 may, for example, tell us we are no longer condemned, we can still, at times, fear God's punishment. As James talks about doubt blowing us about (James 1:6), until we are fully mature there are moments when we allow fear, rather than love, to dominate. The doctrinal truth of us being totally loved by God is proved to us in our experience – much like the love within marriage. While couples take a vow at the start of marriage, their commitment to each other over the years proves their love. Learning to live in a daily relationship of trust and obedience to God allows His love to direct us.

Week Five: Faith and life

Opening Icebreaker

This is a very practical way of showing that faith involves trust – and is also about what we know but cannot see.

Discussion Starters

1. It can be hard for our modern eyes to read the story of Lazarus. He was such a close friend of Jesus', and yet when He heard Lazarus was ill, Jesus stayed where He was for longer – and said that it was for God's glory. He knew the bigger picture in a way that those around Him did not – how hard that must have been for them. Jesus spoke to Martha about being the resurrection and the life – not just in eternity. All life is found and sourced in Him.

2. If we judge our love purely at an emotional level, without regard for the moral obedience that God's Law demands, we may find ourselves excusing what is in fact disobedience, because we still feel warmly towards God. Just because we don't feel self-condemned does not mean that God is excusing our behaviour. We are self-deceived, esteeming our own opinions above God's.

3. Each of the people mentioned in Hebrews stepped out in faith, even though they didn't fully understand what God was asking of them, and wouldn't see or experience the full picture (as is true for all of us, this side of eternity). It is amazing to see how their lives fit into the big story of God's plan though. A great reminder that ours do too!

4. While we can view commands as burdensome, it has been said that God's commands are like the wings that enable us to fly. In complete contrast to the heavy, burdensome rules and regulations the Pharisees were putting on the people, Jesus emphasised love and said that His 'yoke is easy and my burden is light' (Matt. 11:30).

5. Jesus declares that He gives us everlasting life. This provides a real assurance of our salvation, and reminds us that we can experience this eternal life in the here and now.

6. Prayer is the way that God wants us to converse with Him, but there are some things that can hinder this. Here are a few ideas to get you started:

- Unconfessed sin – Psalm 66:18 (but remember 1 John 1:9).
- Interestingly, the way husbands and wives interact with one another can impact prayer – 1 Peter 3:7.
- Unforgiveness – Mark 11:25.
- Not remaining in Christ – John 15:7.
- Asking for something outside of God's will
  – Matthew 6:10; John 15:16; James 4:3.
- Not submitting to Scripture – Proverbs 28:9.
- Doubt – James 1:5–7.

But God wants us to persist in prayer (see the parable of the persistent widow in Luke 18 as well as 1 Thess. 5:17), checking our motives and examining our hearts regularly as we do so.

7. Here are some scriptures to aid your discussion: Mark 1:35; Luke 6:12; Matthew 26:36–46; Hebrews 5:7. Jesus often withdrew in order to pray. He also poured out all of His emotions to God honestly, while still quietly submitting to God's will.

8. As we have seen, verse 15 shows us that God answers prayers. But sometimes we don't see the answer for a long time – or at all. Remind people of how God has an overall plan and the people of faith in Hebrews 11 remained faithful even without seeing all the answers to their prayers. God always responds to prayers aligned to His will, but sometimes there is a spiritual battle going on – look up Daniel 10:12–13 to discuss this concept. Ephesians 6 talks about our spiritual armour, and ends by saying we need to pray in the Spirit always, and keep alert.

Week Six: Be alert

Opening Icebreaker

Stories could be as simple as letting a saucepan boil over and making a mess, or burning dinner because they were distracted. The emphasis is on staying alert. If no one can think of anything, you could discuss how drivers need to stay alert for other road users.

Discussion Starters

1. You could look at what politicians and marketers produce in the name of 'truth' and how popular the phrase 'post-truth' has become. Also how our society allows all kinds of love. If you have time, you may want to move on to discuss whether you think this has affected the Church's views.

2. There may be times when we find it difficult to obey. In those moments we need to remind ourselves that love is the basis of obedience. Meditating on the truth about the cross, and the fact that God loved us from the beginning of time, is so vital. Daily Bible reading, through which we feed our minds with truth, is a great way of living consistently. As is submitting to God's discipline (Heb. 12:10–11), and not always running from difficulties (1 Pet. 1:3–9) as these can be ways in which God is refining us.

3. While our works are not the means of our salvation (the one who loses everything in the flames in 1 Cor. is still saved), the Bible does teach that there will be rewards in this life and our eternal life with Him. Ask the group to discuss how this makes them feel – whether it motivates or worries them.

4. False teachers will probably seem sincere and genuine, especially if they originated in a church. They may have been influenced by worldly culture – and we can be too. New teaching, especially the kind which requires little effort from us, can seem attractive. That's why we have these letters warning us against it!

5. Here Jesus teaches about false prophets, indicating that the fruit in a person's life will reveal who they truly are. We have already seen how the devil likes to counterfeit what Jesus did, so even though some will perform miracles, because they are not walking in the will of God they aren't truly His disciples. Without a relationship with Jesus, we cannot enter eternal life with Him.

6. We can guard against false teaching through careful and consistent study of the Word of God (see 2 Tim. 2:15), by learning to listen closely to the Holy Spirit, looking out for one another, looking at the character and fruit of those purporting to be teachers and through prayer. Colossians 4:2 has a great message: 'Devote yourselves to prayer, being watchful and thankful'. Ephesians 6 teaches us that we are in a battle, and need the armour of God. We are to be attentive and wise, but not allow ourselves to be fearful – as we saw in last week's passage, Jesus has overcome!

7. The main message throughout these letters is to love God and the way we do that is through loving one another. In Colossians 4:6, we are encouraged to let our 'conversation be always full of grace'. While we should never give up ground concerning issues of salvation, making other issues (perhaps such as the way we like to express worship) a cause for division is not showing God's love to one another.

8. Talk about the fact that it is only face to face that we can fully read someone's body language and hear their tone of expression. Taking the time to meet up face to face shows that we are prioritising loving one another.

Week Seven: Stay faithful

Opening Icebreaker
This is simply to start talking about how faithfulness cultivates love, kindness and a sense of wellbeing between those on both the giving and receiving ends.

Discussion Starters
1. We can keep ourselves spiritually fit through feeding daily on the Word, in prayer and fellowship with other believers, but we can also keep physically fit by being aware of our diet and the lifestyle we lead. In both instances it's about taking in the good and then actively using it, rather than overindulging in things that don't do us any good. Let's also remember to rest. Here are some scriptures you might like to use to facilitate discussion: Proverbs 3:7–8; Romans 12:1–2; 1 Corinthians 6:10–20; 9:24–27; 10:31; 1 Timothy 4:8; Ephesians 5:18 and Matthew 11:28.

2. The Bible clearly states that hospitality is something we should be prioritising in our lives and is also a measure of character (possibly because it necessitates putting others first). Here is a small sample of scriptures you might like to look up together: Romans 12:13; 1 Timothy 3:2; 5:3–10; Hebrews 13:2 and 1 Peter 4:8–10.

3. This question has been left deliberately vague as you may want to discuss what qualities a leader should have, people's experiences of leadership and how congregations treat their leaders.

Here are some ideas: Jesus is the head of the Church (see 1 Cor. 4:11), and true Christian leadership will reflect this, laying down personal ambition and becoming a servant, as Jesus did (see Matt. 20:28; Mark 10:45; John 13:1–17). Leaders are also to be examples to their congregation (1 Pet. 5:1–4). There is also a responsibility upon the congregation to humbly submit to leadership (see Heb. 13:17). Of course, all teaching should be subjected to the plumb line of the Word of God. We are also to have the right attitude towards serving one another (you may like to discuss Phil. 2:1–11).

4. A leader who is becoming dictatorial will talk about themselves a lot, condemn those who do not agree with everything they say and label others in a judgmental way. I do not believe that we should submit to domineering leadership without speaking out. Hopefully leaders have people around them who they allow to speak into their lives – who will point out any errors as Galatians 6:1 indicate. But, if not, the Bible does have clear instructions on what to do (1 Tim. 5:19–21).

5. Facilitate an open discussion about what your church does well and what it could do better. This week, you could challenge people to pray for your church leaders daily, and to show they appreciate them in a practical way.

6. While we have not seen God face to face, Jesus was the Word in flesh who dwelt among humans (as John has been at pains to emphasise) and is reigning on the throne today. He continues to show us who God is. But, as we have seen throughout history, those who are evil have not recognised Him for who He truly is. They choose not to 'see' Him.

7. Examples such as Demetrius, and indeed Paul (who was very open about his credentials but also his mistakes),

are provided not for us to compare ourselves to and feel condemned (Rom. 8:1), but to encourage and motivate us to 'press on toward the goal to win the prize' (Phil. 3:14; see also Heb. 10:24–25). We should also find the same encouragement in one another.

8. Give some space and time for reflection and then encourage a time of prayer.

The *Cover to Cover* Bible Study Series

1 Corinthians ✓
Growing a Spirit-filled church
ISBN: 978-1-85345-374-8

2 Corinthians ✓
Restoring harmony
ISBN: 978-1-85345-551-3

1,2,3 John ✓✓✓
Walking in the truth
ISBN: 978-1-78259-763-6

1 Peter ✓
Good reasons for hope
ISBN: 978-1-78259-088-0

2 Peter ✓
Living in the light of God's promises
ISBN: 978-1-78259-403-1

23rd Psalm
The Lord is my shepherd
ISBN: 978-1-85345-449-3

1 Timothy ✓
Healthy churches – effective Christians
ISBN: 978-1-85345-291-8

2 Timothy and Titus ✓✓
Vital Christianity
ISBN: 978-1-85345-338-0

Abraham
Adventures of faith
ISBN: 978-1-78259-089-7

Acts 1-12 ✓
Church on the move
ISBN: 978-1-85345-574-2

Acts 13-28 ✓
To the ends of the earth
ISBN: 978-1-85345-592-6

Barnabas
Son of encouragement
ISBN: 978-1-85345-911-5

Bible Genres
Hearing what the Bible really says
ISBN: 978-1-85345-987-0

Daniel ✓
Living boldly for God
ISBN: 978-1-85345-986-3

David
A man after God's own heart
ISBN: 978-1-78259-444-4

Ecclesiastes ✓
Hard questions and spiritual answers
ISBN: 978-1-85345-371-7

Elijah ✓
A man and his God
ISBN: 978-1-85345-575-9

Elisha ✓
A lesson in faithfulness
ISBN: 978-1-78259-494-9

Ephesians ✓
Claiming your inheritance
ISBN: 978-1-85345-229-1

Esther ✓
For such a time as this
ISBN: 978-1-85345-511-7

Ezekiel ✓
A prophet for all times
ISBN: 978-1-78259-836-7

Fruit of the Spirit
Growing more like Jesus
ISBN: 978-1-85345-375-5

Galatians ✓
Freedom in Christ
ISBN: 978-1-85345-648-0

Genesis 1-11 ✓
Foundations of reality
ISBN: 978-1-85345-404-2

Genesis 12-50 ✓
Founding fathers of faith
ISBN: 978-1-78259-960-9

God's Rescue Plan
Finding God's fingerprints on human history
ISBN: 978-1-85345-294-9

Great Prayers of the Bible
Applying them to our lives today
ISBN: 978-1-85345-253-6

Habakkuk ✓
Choosing God's way
ISBN: 978-1-78259-843-5

Haggai ✓
Motivating God's people
ISBN: 978-1-78259-686-8

Hebrews ✓
Jesus – simply the best
ISBN: 978-1-85345-337-3

Isaiah 1-39 ✓
Prophet to the nations
ISBN: 978-1-85345-510-0

Isaiah 40-66 ✓
Prophet of restoration
ISBN: 978-1-85345-550-6

For current prices or to order, visit **cwr.org.uk/shop**
Available online or from Christian bookshops.

Be inspired by God.
Every day.

Confidently face life's challenges by equipping yourself daily with God's Word. There is something for everyone...

Every Day with Jesus

Selwyn Hughes' renowned writing is updated by Mick Brooks into these trusted and popular notes.

Life Every Day

Jeff Lucas helps apply the Bible to daily life with his trademark humour and insight.

Inspiring Women
Every Day

Encouragement, uplifting scriptures and insightful daily thoughts for women.

The Manual

Straight-talking guides to help men walk daily with God. Written by Carl Beech.

To find out more about all our daily Bible reading notes, or to take out a subscription, visit **cwr.org.uk/biblenotes** or call 01252 784700.
Also available in Christian bookshops.

 Printed format  Large print format Email format Ebook format

SmallGroup central

All of our small group ideas and resources in one place

Online:

smallgroupcentral.org.uk
is filled with free video teaching, tools, articles and a whole host of ideas.

On the road:

A range of seminars themed for small groups can be brought to your local community. Contact us at **hello@smallgroupcentral.org.uk**

In print:

Books, study guides and DVDs covering an extensive list of themes, Bible books and life issues.

Find out more at:
smallgroupcentral.org.uk

Courses and events

Waverley Abbey College

Publishing and media

Conference facilities

Transforming lives

CWR's vision is to enable people to experience personal transformation through applying God's Word to their lives and relationships.

Our Bible-based training and resources help people around the world to:
• Grow in their walk with God
• Understand and apply Scripture to their lives
• Resource themselves and their church
• Develop pastoral care and counselling skills
• Train for leadership
• Strengthen relationships, marriage and family life and much more.

Our insightful writers provide daily Bible reading notes and other resources for all ages, and our experienced course designers and presenters have gained an international reputation for excellence and effectiveness.

CWR's Training and Conference Centre in Surrey, England, provides excellent facilities in an idyllic setting – ideal for both learning and spiritual refreshment.

CWR Applying God's Word
to everyday life and relationships

CWR, Waverley Abbey House,
Waverley Lane, Farnham,
Surrey GU9 8EP, UK

Telephone: +44 (0)1252 784700
Email: info@cwr.org.uk
Website: cwr.org.uk

Registered Charity No. 294387
Company Registration No. 1990308